DISPROVING GOD

&

5 Adequate Reasons
to Be an Atheist

STAKS ROSCH

With a Foreword by

Herb Silverman

Disproving God & 5 Adequate Reasons to Be an
Atheist

ISBN: 979-8-641-11620-4

DEDICATION

When I started blogging and becoming an activist, there were days that I felt I wasn't making a difference. There were days that I felt no one was hearing my voice. But from across the world in Japan, activist Mieko Terashita heard my voice and supported me. Her support, friendship, and courage inspired me to write and stay active. Sadly, Mieko passed away in April 2019. This book and my activism would not have been possible without her assistance. In her honor, I dedicate this book to her memory. To my readers, let this dedication remind you that if there is someone in your life who has given you support, as Mieko has given me, thank them while they are alive. I only hope she knew how much her encouragement meant to me.

CONTENTS

FOREWORD

The good book (pun intended) or pamphlet that promotes atheism should contain arguments that make sense, acknowledge counterarguments, and counter the counterarguments. Not only does Staks Rosch succeed in this endeavor, but he does it in a way that is not likely to offend open-minded theists. I understand why some atheists take pride in offending religious people, which is counterproductive if you want others to hear and appreciate your point of view.

In plain, easy-to-understand language, Rosch begins with a compelling and deceptively simple case for why there is no God, especially not one with all the attributes most believers assign to their deity. In doing so, it's clear that he has read and understood the Bible better than most who profess belief in all its contents.

After disposing of traditional gods, Rosch then makes an even more compelling case for why it is reasonable to be an atheist. He gives five sufficient reasons and acknowledges that to those five could be added an even higher number of reasons to not believe in a higher power. Without getting into technicalities of science, he points out how commonly accepted scientific findings have now replaced many explanations attributed to God. His arguments are sprinkled with humor that should make believers smile, even as they search for reasons to not accept the reasonable arguments presented.

An advantage to being an atheist (without a belief in any gods) is that we are happy to acknowledge that there are things we don't know and that we enjoy the search for knowledge, wherever it leads. We don't have to defend the indefensible. Rosch empathizes with religious believers who grew up in a religious environment and never stepped outside that narrow box. He gives examples of how accepted beliefs with which a person was raised can seem ridiculous to someone outside that faith. Of course, some people have never read the ridiculous parts that Rosch carefully critiques.

Prolific science writer Isaac Asimov once said, "Properly read, the Bible is the most potent force for atheism ever conceived." Rosch makes that case through excellent and simple arguments for atheism. This is a pamphlet to read and pass on to your friends, whether they be religious or nonreligious.

****

Herb Silverman is the founder of the Secular Coalition for America and author of Candidate without a *Prayer: An Autobiography of a Jewish Atheist in the Bible Belt* and *An Atheist Stranger in a Strange Religious Land.*

ACKNOWLEDGMENTS

A special thank you goes out to my wife, Jenny, for editing this book and for all the other support she has given me. I also want to thank my brother, Michael, for his insights and for our long conversations at White Castle about this book. Lastly, I want to thank all the Dangerous Talkers out there who have listened to my radio show and podcasts and who have read and contributed to my blogs and articles over the years. Thanks to you all.

INTRODUCTION

A number of years ago, when I was a Production Expeditor in a machine shop / weld shop, it came out that I was an atheist. At the time, I was doing atheist activism and the local newspaper did a story on my involvement with one of the local atheist groups. I knew they were writing the story and I expected some backlash, but I just didn't think about how it would affect me at work.

The thing about manufacturing shops in a Republican-controlled Pennsylvania county is that they generally aren't the most progressive of work environments. My bosses were all pretty right-wing, and many of my coworkers were rural hunters—not exactly known for their progressive values. When one of the machinists brought the article to the attention of the entire shop, I suddenly got a little nervous.

To my surprise, many of the people I worked with also didn't believe in God. They never used the word *atheist* before, but they were in fact atheists. They might not have all been the humanistic atheists that I usually interact with, but they were atheists nonetheless.

Still, a small number of coworkers started to avoid me like the plague. When we did have to work together, they put their religion front and center and loudly affirmed their religiosity. One of the office women even told me (not in a joking fashion) that she didn't think the company should reimburse me for expenses because the money says "In God We Trust" on it. When I threatened to take the matter to her supervisor, she did her job and reimbursed me—but she wasn't happy about it.

Many of my religious and even a few of my atheist coworkers enjoyed having religious conversations with me. One guy I worked with quite a lot was a Mennonite. He was one of those people who wouldn't let his kids read the Harry Potter books because he believed they promoted witchcraft. Because of the nature of our workplace environment, it was perfectly fine for me to laugh at him and point out just how silly that was. Playful banter and teasing were commonplace in our shop, and everyone had insulting nicknames. We all had our buttons pushed. The "Harry Potter is of the devil" joke rarely got old.

Our shop worked with many other local shops, and one aspect of my job was dealing with outside vendors. Their representatives would often see me, or I would visit their shops for parts. Before long, my atheism became quite well known to many of them.

One vendor was very religious and truly enjoyed having conversations with me on the subject matter. He was always very polite and kind, and our conversations were rarely antagonistic.

There was, however, another vendor whose shop I visited quite often who was a Promise Keeper and a very religious right-wing Republican. Whenever I stopped by, he would always start talking to me about politics and/or religion. While we would tease each other and have antagonistic discussions on these topics, we both enjoyed the conversations. I even lost a bet with him about the Bush/Kerry presidential election. The day after the election, McDonald's was on me.

I was surprised when one year, right before Christmas, he had a present for me. I saw it as a thoughtful gesture even though I am not sure if that was his intent or if he thought of it more as a gag gift. It was the book *The Case for Christ* by Lee Strobel.

I think he might have been surprised that I actually thanked him for the gift and took the time to read it. A few months later, I came back to him and discussed several of the points made in the book and why they were problematic.

The following year, I thought it might be nice to return the favor. When shopping around for a good atheist book to give to a Christian, there are some important things to consider.

First and foremost was length. I was worried that if I gave him a book that was too long or looked too thick, he might not even bother to read it. I wanted something short, to the point, and not intimidating.

Second, I was looking for was a book that actually conveyed some quality information and made great arguments.

And third, I wanted a book written for Christians.

There was only one book that I knew of at the time that fit those criteria—Sam Harris's *A Letter to a Christian Nation*.

But while I took the time to read my friend's gift, he did not do the same, despite the fact that my gift was half the length of his. I purposefully picked it because it was short, and he still didn't bother to read it.

Sam Harris isn't known for wearing kid gloves when it comes to religious sensibilities, but the title of his book might not have been antagonistic enough. It was a letter to Christians from a prominent atheist. Maybe my vendor friend just didn't want to read a letter from an atheist. That's why I have titled the first section of this book "A Simple Argument for Disproving God."

The argument is simple and not very intimidating. Still, I am making a bold claim here. I am claiming to disprove the existence of a deity. That's a challenge. I am throwing down the gauntlet and daring religious believers. But more than that, I am taking on the traditional atheist status quo that you can't prove a negative.

We atheists tend to overclarify that when we say that we don't believe in any gods, we aren't saying with absolute certainty that we *know* that gods don't exist.

This is all very true, but it plays into the language game of many religious believers. This is why I often point out that there is a difference between knowing something with absolute certainty and knowing something with reasonable certainty.

For all practical purposes, no one really cares about absolute certainty. That is more of a philosophical distraction. No one says that Santa Claus might exist or that no one can disprove the existence of unicorns. While it is true that we can't say with absolute certainty that old Saint Nick and little Uni from the *Dungeons & Dragons* cartoon don't exist, no one is seriously going to argue that they do. In the same vein, I have no qualms about making the claim that God is a fictional character who does not exist.

Unfortunately, that will not satisfy my religious critics, so the first section of this pamphlet focuses on a philosophical argument I created that disproves the existence of God on a more fundamental level.

I originally created this argument to win a video contest sponsored by Sam Harris's Project Reason foundation. While it didn't win the prize, I received a lot of interesting feedback from critics. I took some of that feedback to heart and tweaked the argument to make it stronger for this pamphlet. I also added some Bible quotations for Christians that support my argument that God does not exist.

That's pretty amazing, right? I actually quote the Bible to disprove the existence of God. Still, even if you consider that to be "cherry-picking" or the devil's use of Scripture to lead Christians astray, the argument works just as well without the Bible quotations.

I merely use them for additional support. In other words, this argument should work against any god. So if you are a Muslim, Jew, or other theist, this argument should disprove your god too.

The second essay in this pamphlet is titled "5 Adequate Reasons to Be an Atheist." Based on a *Huffington Post* article I wrote ("Five Pretty Good Reasons to Be an Atheist"), this is a more lighthearted piece. It still presents some pretty hard-hitting arguments, but it does so in a more enjoyable way. The first essay is a bit academic for some, so I thought it would be a good idea to pair it with something a bit humorous.

It is one thing to disprove God, but why should someone be an atheist? I picked five adequate reasons for being an atheist, but that doesn't necessarily mean they are the best or the only reasons. For one thing, everyone is different, and some reasons resonate with some people better than they resonate with others. So that is one reason why I am not claiming that these are the best reasons.

There are also many more than just five reasons to be an atheist. Five is a good number, though. I like five. Five isn't as short as three, but it's still not as intimidating as ten. There are too many lists with ten, and I didn't want to risk the comparison to the Ten Commandments. I had thought about four, because nobody really uses four, but ultimately I went with five. Like I said, five is a good number.

Whether you like the more academic, logical proof of the first part of the book or the more lighthearted approach of the second half, there is something for every theist and atheist.

Enjoy!

A SIMPLE ARGUMENT
DISPROVING GOD

There I was, outside of a Christians in Action meeting on a pleasant Thursday evening during my freshman year of college. Around me were several Christians engaged in friendly conversation about our clashing worldviews. The conversation was light and jovial, but everyone was quite passionate about what they believed—or in my case, what I didn't believe. We all advocated for our positions with a fire in our bellies, as the saying goes.

As "the atheist" on campus, I was in what some might call enemy territory. But I didn't see it that way at all. The Christians I was bantering with were my friends, and we were all enjoying the spirited discourse (pun intended). For a moment, I felt a little like a celebrity. It was not often that I got to be the center of attention in this manner. When my Christian friend had asked me to attend the meeting with an open heart and an open mind, I couldn't refuse.

On this autumn evening, I had the opportunity to philosophize with religious fundamentalists for the first time in my life. I had never met anyone who held such obviously ridiculous beliefs before, and I was very curious as to why they held these beliefs. What were their reasons? This, above all else, kept me engaged with them. They too were curious about my lack of belief in a deity. They had never met an open and vocal atheist before, and it was this mutual curiosity that became the backbone of our friendships.

The year was 1994. It was well before thirty thousand atheists gathered in the rain at the first Reason Rally on the National Mall in Washington, DC. It was before Harris, Dawkins, Hitchens, and Dennett kicked off the "New Atheism" movement with their bestselling books. Even the internet was new, and so the atheist online community was practically nonexistent. While there were atheist organizations, I didn't know of them at the time. For all practical purposes, I was on my own, reinventing the wheels of reason. I had to discover arguments and counterarguments that I later learned had been around for centuries and even millennia. When a Christian would hit me with the first-cause argument, I had to think about it. I didn't know there were books on this stuff already. I only realized that others had written about these issues when I took an Introduction to Philosophy class a year later.

Out of all the questions my Christian friends demanded that I answer, there was one that I struggled with for a very long time. Even after I got my master's degree in philosophy, I still hadn't found anyone who I thought had a satisfying answer to this question. Most of my fellow atheists have a pretty standard response to it, which isn't terrible, but it won't satisfy any fundamentalist Christian.

The question that my Christian friends asked me that evening—and that has been asked of me by many other religious believers since—was this: Can you disprove the existence of God?

Now, the obvious response is that the question itself is in question. The burden of proof is obviously on the person who asserts a claim and not the person who lacks a belief in the asserted claim. We could, of course, ask if anyone could present evidence that disproves the existence of Darth Vader. Even though we all know that George Lucas made him up and that we have his firsthand testimony of that, this still doesn't completely disprove Darth Vader's existence. For all we know, Lucas could have built a super-telescope in his backyard that enabled him to see events that occurred a long time ago in a galaxy far, far away. He might just be reporting those events to us or using that knowledge as inspiration for his stories. Perhaps the Force is strong with him and he is sensing Vader's thoughts and experiences unknowingly. We might want to consider creating a group of Star Wars scholars called "The Vader Seminar" to learn more about the historical Darth Vader.

The "burden of proof" response to the question of disproving God is a perfectly valid response. The fact is that the burden of proof really is on those who assert a belief in a deity. An atheist doesn't have any obligation to disprove any deity at all. Even if I were to assert the claim that gods do not exist, I don't think I would be under any obligation to disprove the existence of every possible deity. I would be required to point out that no valid evidence has been put forward to support the assertion of any deities.

While absence of evidence isn't evidence of absence necessarily, without valid evidence, there is no reason to accept the proposition on face value. It all depends on the claim being asserted. The more extraordinary the claim, the more likely I am to expect evidence for that claim. If one of my Christian friends asserted that she got a passing grade in biology despite her belief in biblical creationism, I might demand evidence of that, but if she couldn't provide that evidence, I would probably accept that the absence of that evidence was not evidence of absence in relation to her passing grade in biology because unfortunately people do pass biology classes on the university level even if they reject the science of evolution in favor of biblical creationism. It's just a sad fact of our education system.

Accepting someone's claim of passing biology despite the absence of valid evidence is different, however, from accepting someone's claim of the existence of a deity despite the absence of valid evidence. One is much more plausible than the other.

Still, despite the fact that the burden of proof remains with those claiming that their deity of choice exists, pointing this out to fundamentalist believers will rarely convince them that their question is faulty. Religious believers still want atheists to disprove their deity.

Let me speak frankly here. I think that religion is bullshit and that no deities exist. To my knowledge, no one in all of recorded history has ever presented any valid and/or credible evidence that supports the assertion that his or her deity or any other deity actually exists.

Sure, believers can talk about the beauty in a sunrise or the love we humans feel for each other, but all those things have scientific explanations that don't include a deity. Bill O'Reilly's 2001 argument on *The O'Reilly Factor* that the "tides go in and the tides go out," implying an existent God as the cause, actually does have a pretty well-known explanation. God, on the other hand, does not have a shred of evidence supporting his existence. In fact, there is a strong and yet simple argument that does disprove the existence of God.

The best part about this argument that disproves the existence of God is that it can sometimes be delivered in less than a minute. This means it is a quick and easy argument that can be presented in a short conversation. Also, it isn't just geared toward fundamentalist religious believers. It is an argument that can apply to many conceptions of God—even metaphorical and vague conceptions.

Pre-premise

The pre-premise of the argument is simply a definition of God. One problem I often have with religious believers—even those of the same religion—is that nearly everyone has a different conception of who and even what God is. So let's define God in a pretty broad fashion before the argument even begins. I'll assign four basic attributes to God:

1. God is supernatural.
2. God is all-knowing.
3. God is all-powerful.
4. God is all-loving.

I don't anticipate any objections to this four-part definition, but don't take my word for it; be skeptical! Let's look at what the Bible says about this four-part definition. Is God supernatural? According to Genesis 1:1 in the King James Version, "In the beginning God created the heaven and the earth." It seems to me that according to the Bible, God created nature and is therefore supernatural.

In the New Testament, John 4:24 says, "God [is] a Spirit: and they that worship him must worship [him] in spirit and in truth." That sounds a little supernatural to me. Aside from alcohol, there are no spirits in nature . . . and I don't think that is what John had in mind when he talked about worshipping God in spirit.

Is God all-knowing according to the Bible? Hebrews 4:13 says, "Neither is there any creature that is not manifest in his sight: but all things are naked and opened unto the eyes of him with whom we have to do."

That's a little vague, so a religious believer might not be convinced that the God they worship is actually all-knowing, but according to Psalm 147:5, "Great is our Lord, and of great power: his understanding is infinite."

A religious believer would have a hard time arguing that infinite understanding could not be equated to being all-knowing, and it is highly unlikely that a religious believer would argue with an atheist's claim that the Bible supports the view that God is all-knowing. But just to be crystal clear about this, 1 John 3:20 says, "For if our heart condemn us, God is greater than our heart, and knoweth all things." So there it is: God knoweth all things, except that in nearly two thousand years, "knoweth" wouldn't be recognized by spell-check.

Is God all-powerful according to the Bible? Job seemed to think so. He said in the book bearing his name, "I know that thou canst do every thing, and that no thought can be withholden from thee" (Job 42:2). But what does Job know anyway? Jeremiah, on the other hand, claims to have heard from God personally. In fact, God boasted it to Jeremiah in verses 32:26–27: "Then came the word of the LORD unto Jeremiah, saying, Behold, I am the LORD, the God of all flesh: is there any thing too hard for me?"

Romans 9:21 also makes a solid argument for God's omnipotence: "Hath not the potter power over the clay, of the same lump to make one vessel unto honour, and another unto dishonour?" That's sound reasoning indeed that God is all-powerful, but we have yet to hear Jesus weigh in on this. Matthew 19:26 claims, "Jesus beheld them, and said unto them, with men this is impossible; but with God all things are possible." Let me be clear here: with God all things are possible according to the Bible.

Last, and probably most significant, is God all-loving? Well, that is a tricky one. I doubt many believers will argue that he isn't all-loving at this point, but this tends to be the one thing they take issue with after the fact. What I mean is that after the argument is over and God has been disproven, they tend to reject this part of the definition in order to hold on to their belief in God in the face of just having had their God disproven right before their eyes.

Still, it is hard to find biblical support for the view that God is all-loving. In fact, quite a few passages talk about attributes of people and people themselves that God hates. I won't go into detail about that because it isn't relevant to this argument. There are a few passages, however, that might be interpreted in a way that supports the view that God is all-loving.

Romans 8:38–39 talks about the love of God in this way: "For I am persuaded, that neither death, nor life, nor angels, nor principalities, nor powers, nor things present, nor things to come, nor height, nor depth, nor any other creature, shall be able to separate us from the love of God, which is in Christ Jesus our Lord."

But the real argument in favor of God being all-loving comes from the biblical view that human beings are basically the scum of the earth. Yes, the biblical view is that humans are so horrible that we deserve to be tortured for all eternity. Not only that, but we are so wretched and vile that nothing could love us . . . except God, because he is all-loving. God is so all-loving that he even loves us despite the fact that we are the vilest creatures: "But God commendeth his love toward us, in that, while we were yet sinners, Christ died for us" (Romans 5:8). This is often referred to by religious believers as "God's grace." This message is also crystalized in the famous verse John 3:16: "For God so loved the world, that he gave his only begotten Son, that whosoever believeth in him should not perish, but have everlasting life."

If God loved the world, the argument could be made that he is all-loving. But here is the problem. It isn't just that those who believe get a reward; those who don't believe are condemned: "He that believeth on him is not condemned: but he that believeth not is condemned already, because he hath not believed in the name of the only begotten Son of God" (John 3:18). The idea is that God doesn't want us to be condemned, "for God sent not his Son into the world to condemn the world; but that the world through him might be saved" (John 3:17). Christians often talk about how God wants a relationship with people through Jesus. This is an important point that I want to return to later in the argument. For now, I think I have shown that there is at least some biblical support for the claim that God is love, as 1 John 4:7–8 puts it: "Beloved, let us love one another: for love is of God; and every one that loveth is born of God, and knoweth God. He that loveth not knoweth not God; for God is love."

Premise 1

Now that we have the definition of God squared away, let's move on to the meat of the argument. Religious believers often ask me what it would take to convince me that God exists. I think this is a really good question, and I am not sure I have an answer for it. But I do know who might have an answer, if he actually existed: God.

The first premise of the argument is this: If God is all-knowing, then God would know the precise evidence required to convince me that God exists.

"The LORD knoweth the thoughts of man, that they are vanity," according to Psalm 94:11. Psalm 139:2 says, "Thou knowest my downsitting and mine uprising, thou understandest my thought afar off." And Luke 16:15 states, "And he said unto them, Ye are they which justify yourselves before men; but God knoweth your hearts: for that which is highly esteemed among men is abomination in the sight of God."

God allegedly knows my thoughts, understands my thoughts, and knows my heart. So it stands to reason that God would know the precise evidence required to convince me that God exists.

Premise 2

Knowing something and being able to do something about that knowledge are two entirely different things. Just because God knows what would convince me of his existence doesn't mean he necessarily has the power to do something with that knowledge. Except in this case, it does mean that.

The second premise of the argument is just that: if God is all-powerful, then God could present the precise evidence required to convince me that God exists.

It isn't just that many religious believers believe that God intervenes in this world through miracles and such, but according to our definition, God is all-powerful, so he would have the power to intervene in this world if he so chooses. Presenting me—or anyone else, for that matter—with convincing evidence is certainly something that an all-powerful deity should be able to do.

According to the Bible, God presented evidence of his existence to people all the time. He burned bushes and stopped the sun from moving, and Jesus even allowed Thomas to poke his wounds after his resurrection: "Then saith he to Thomas, Reach hither thy finger, and behold my hands; and reach hither thy hand, and thrust it into my side: and be not faithless, but believing. And Thomas answered and said unto him, My LORD and my God. Jesus saith unto him, Thomas, because thou hast seen me, thou hast believed: blessed are they that have not seen, and yet have believed. And many other signs truly did Jesus in the presence of his disciples, which are not written in this book" (John 20:27–30).

Premise 3

Just because we can do something does not mean that we must do that thing. God might know how to convince me and he might be able to convince me, but does that mean that he would actually want to convince me? Actually, in this case, yes, he would.

The third premise of the argument again follows from the definition we laid out: If God is all-loving, then God should desire to present the precise evidence required to convince me that God exists.

Proverbs 8:17 says, "I love them that love me; and those that seek me early shall find me." I actually remember one of my Christian friends from Christians in Action challenging me with this verse during my freshmen year of college. It wasn't just any Christian friend either. It was a student a few years older than I was, whom I greatly respected. In a sense, this friend was a mentor to me despite the fact that we disagreed on the very issue he was mentoring me about.

I often took long late-night walks during my early college years that sometimes stretched into the early morning hours. And on one such walk, when no one was around, I took my mentor's advice: as genuinely as I could, I called out to God. I wanted to seek him out. I wanted to know. If there was a truth to be found, I genuinely wanted to find it. It was early in the morning. I actually sought him out "early" just as the Bible instructed. A few years later, I even humbled myself enough to try this again at the request of yet another close Christian friend.

You cannot be all-loving from a distance. That is an unrequited love, and that just doesn't seem to fit with the character of God we established in the definition. God wants to save people through Jesus Christ. So it necessarily follows that he would desire a personal and intimate relationship with all people.

Premise 4

The fourth and final premise is simply this: atheists exist! I lack a belief in deities and I exist. I think therefore I am. I do not just lack a belief in gods; I am reasonably certain (although that certainty could be shaken with convincing evidence) that no gods exist and that the biblical God in particular does not exist. I remain unconvinced about the God proposition.

If the fact that I am living proof is not enough for you, consider this: even the Bible admits that atheists exist. Fundamentalist Christians quote Psalm 14:1–3 to me all the time: "The fool hath said in his heart, There is no God. They are corrupt, they have done abominable works, there is none that doeth good. The LORD looked down from heaven upon the children of men, to see if there were any that did understand, and seek God. They are all gone aside, they are all together become filthy: there is none that doeth good, no, not one." According to the Bible, I am a fool for not believing in God, but at least the Bible admits that there are people who do not believe. Name-calling aside, that is really the point here. According to the Bible, God does believe in the existence of atheists.

Conclusion

Finally, based on the definition of God laid out in the pre-premise and on the premises themselves, the conclusion is clear: God cannot exist. Let me summarize the argument.

We define God with the following attributes:

1. God is supernatural.
2. God is all-knowing.
3. God is all-powerful.
4. God is all-loving.

If God is all-knowing, then God would know the precise evidence required to convince me that God exists. If God is all-powerful, then God could present the precise evidence required to convince me that God exists. If God is all-loving, then God should desire to present the precise evidence required to convince me that God exists. Atheists exist! Therefore, God cannot exist.

5 ADEQUATE REASONS TO BE AN ATHEIST

People love lists, am I right? Here is a list of five pretty adequate reasons you should be an atheist. I can't say they are the best reasons because that all depends on the type of theist you are and the level of conditioning and indoctrination you have received throughout your life.

I know I am not going to convince everyone with this list because, for most religious believers, god-belief has been preached to them from before they could walk like a biblical serpent or talk like a burning bush.

Then there is the religious conditioning that has pervaded our society. There is a reason religious beliefs are so "deeply held." And there is a reason people take any criticism of their deeply held religious beliefs as a personal attack rather than mere skepticism of an idea. That reason is the early indoctrination most people are exposed to in our culture. It is this knee-jerk reaction to any doubt, questioning, or challenging of religious beliefs that closes people's minds off to reason and critical thinking on the subject.

Many devout religious believers mistakenly think that they were once atheists in the same sense that I am an atheist. And they often flaunt their former lack of belief in an attempt to gain credibility with vocal atheist activists like me. While they may have been an atheist in the sense of merely lacking a belief in any deities, few actually thought about and researched the arguments for and against various deities the way I have or other atheist activists have.

The reality of the situation is that most religious believers who claim to be former atheists were indoctrinated into a particular belief, rebelled against that belief, and then fell victim to religious persuasion sparked by a traumatic situation. This influence ignited the old inculcation, causing the person to develop a fiery passion for Jesus . . . or L. Ron Hubbard, Mohammad, or some other religious figure.

Probably not Oden, though. No one worships Oden anymore, despite the fact that Norse legend says that Oden defeated all the Frost Giants, and you don't see any Frost Giants roaming around, do you?

In any case, the following are five adequate reasons you might want to ponder and consider that might challenge you to rethink your deeply held faith-based convictions and become an atheist—if you can get past your knee-jerk reaction of being offended that someone might not believe in the same beliefs you do based on insufficient evidence.

1. We Don't Need No Stinkin' Deities

Ever since the enlightenment, religions have been fighting a losing battle against science. The need for gods and supernatural explanations has moved more and more to the gaps of human knowledge and understanding.

There was a time when, if humanity didn't know the answer to one of life's questions, then people would make up a supernatural explanation or simply assign that explanation to a deity. That time, unfortunately, is still the present.

There are surprisingly still a lot of people who claim that God cures cancer when someone's cancer goes into remission or that God is looking out for them if they happen to survive a horrible accident that kills everyone else.

While those may sound like extreme examples, sadly, they are all too common. Whenever there are hurricanes, tornados, or earthquakes, there will usually be some religious leader blaming some group he or she doesn't like for bringing God's wrath down upon the world.

Survivors will praise God for sparing them as others are still lying on the ground dead or in hospitals dying. Even CNN anchor Wolf Blitzer asked a tornado survivor if she praised God for her survival. When she famously said no, "I'm actually an atheist," Blitzer was dumbfounded.

There was a time when people didn't know about germs and viruses. There was a time when we didn't have five-day weather forecasts. There was a time when we didn't understand just how large the universe truly is. In those times, it was easy for people to turn to the supernatural in order to explain things in the world around them that they didn't understand. Now we have science.

Science may not have all the answers to all the questions, but through science, we are learning more and more of those answers and asking questions we never even thought to ask before. As it turns out, as we learn more and more, God seems to be the answer to none of our questions. He's simply the temporary placeholder before we inevitably discover the real answers.

Evolution through natural selection has explained how human beings evolved over time from a common ancestry of other primates. The discovery of natural selection as the mechanism for evolutionary change closed a huge gap in our understanding, a gap previously filled by God. This is why so many religious believers reject the science of evolution despite the ridiculous mountains of evidence in support of this massively supported scientific theory.

Unfortunately, this is probably where I lose many religious believers. Yes, evolution is a scientific theory, but when scientists apply the word *theory*, it means a well-substantiated explanation that has been repeatedly tested and confirmed through scientific observations and experimentation. In other words, evolution is a fact. It happened, and in the words of Wolf Blitzer, it is happening now.

Then there is the big bang theory, which explains the origin of the universe itself. While of course some religious believers are still in denial that the big bang occurred, despite all the evidence in support of it, there are some religious believers out there who credit God for causing the big bang in the first place.

Even though the big bang closes off another huge gap in our understanding that was previously attributed to God, religious believers are attempting to either pretend that it didn't happen at all or minimize the size of the gap to allow God to continue to creep through. Either way, it is clear that scientific understanding minimizes the need for supernatural explanations.

As we learn more through science, God's role will no doubt become even more marginalized, even for religious believers. The fact is that there really is no role for a deity to play at all. We can just factor out the deity and focus on finding the true scientific explanations and answers.

Instead of assigning supernatural explanations to things we don't yet understand, we can simply admit that we don't understand why something is the way it is and then endeavor to understand it better. We don't need to plug our ignorance with deities anymore.

Spiritual guru Deepak Chopra issued a million-dollar challenge to any atheist who could explain how thoughts happen from a materialistic cause. His premise was that because scientists can't explain it, God must be the answer. This, however, only shows his own failure to admit ignorance. At the time of the writing of this book, scientists don't know how thoughts happen inside the brain. So what? That doesn't mean that a deity does it. It just means that scientists have not yet figured it out and can comfortably admit a temporary lack of knowledge. We don't need a deity as an explanation. We can admit that we don't yet have an explanation and keep looking.

2. The Problem of Evil

Is God willing to prevent evil, but not able? Then he is not omnipotent. Is he able, but not willing? Then he is malevolent. Is he both able and willing? Then whence cometh evil? Is he neither able nor willing? Then why call him God?

—Epicurus (341–270 BCE)

Epicurus asked those questions a long time ago, and we have yet to hear a valid response from religious leaders. The most common religious responses to this problem are poor and inadequate.

The two responses I hear most are that God gave man "free will" and that suffering is all part of God's plan, which promises ultimate justice at some future date. But upon even the mildest scrutiny, these justifications fall apart horribly.

My alleged "free will" doesn't cause hurricanes, earthquakes, and/or tornadoes, nor does God's alleged "ultimate justice" justify any of the horrible suffering and death that people face around the world on a daily basis.

One doesn't have to go to Africa to see children starving needlessly. There are children starving needlessly in the richest nations in the world. And did those kids (either here or in Africa) offend God in some way? Perhaps those kids need to suffer horribly and die to teach us something important about ourselves. Obviously those children are just props being used by God to teach us charity or something, right? That truly would be egotistical, wouldn't it?

Think about it. God causes or allows for kids to suffer and die just so you can learn to give the price of a cup of coffee a day to charity. You must be so special. How many children had to suffer and die so that you could learn God's special message that was so important that he couldn't beam it directly into your brain?

What about all the people who have cancer? Does God have his reasons for torturing them? Is there some sort of divine plan for them to suffer horribly and die young? And what about the people who have to watch as their loved one withers away from the ravages of cancer and other diseases? They suffer too, and that suffering isn't caused by their alleged "free will." If there is some divine reason for their suffering, I would very much like to know what that reason could possibly be, because it just seems needlessly cruel for an all-powerful and all-benevolent deity to do something like that.

Perhaps if only non-Christians got cancer, Christians could make the argument that cancer could be a punishment for unbelief, but that isn't the case. As a point of fact, Christians get cancer at the exact same rate as non-Christians. Cancer—like every other disease—affects people of all religions and no religion completely indiscriminately. This is just one reason the "problem of evil" continues to be an adequate reason to be an atheist.

3. Oh, Hell!

I can understand why so many religious believers want to write off the Old Testament with all its barbarism and rules, like don't eat shellfish, don't wear mixed clothing, don't get divorced, don't spill your seed, don't be gay, don't call a priest "baldy," and so on. But then there are the things you must do, like stone disobedient children, marry the man who raped you, treat your Hebrew slaves well, and bury your shit in the woods. All the smiting, stoning, raping, and pillaging can also be a little hard for our modern sense of morality to stomach.

So I understand why many religious believers want to distance themselves from all that by pointing out that Jesus created a new covenant, and therefore, the Old Testament rules no longer apply. What I can't understand is why so few religious believers are out there trying to distance themselves from the New Testament.

Sure, Jesus said some pretty cool things in the New Testament, like turn the other cheek and judge not lest ye be judged, but he also said some pretty horrific things too. As bad as all those Old Testament rules and punishments were, they really don't hold a candle to the horror that is the New Testament.

For one thing, all that Old Testament stuff is temporary. It's just rules and punishments in life. But the New Testament—like any good sequel—has to step up the action a bit. American revolutionary Thomas Paine put it best when he wrote, in a letter to Thomas Erskine, "Of all the tyrannies that affect mankind, tyranny in religion is the worst; every other species of tyranny is limited to the world we live in; but this attempts to stride beyond the grave, and seeks to pursue us into eternity."

The concept of hell is probably one of the most disturbing religious ideas ever conceived by man. It was great to strike fear into the hearts of evildoers back in the day, but today our morality has evolved quite a bit. We no longer view women as property, nor do we consider slavery a valid business model. Most people recognize that torture is wrong. And yet we are expected to believe that some deity will torture us or allow us to be tortured by his inaction for all eternity if we don't believe he exists based on insufficient evidence and worship his virgin-born son?

When you really think about the logistics of hell, it doesn't make much sense. And I'm not just talking about the old internet meme addressing the question of whether hell is exothermic or endothermic.

The thing about eternal torture is that it is supposed to be . . . well, eternal. And as it turns out, eternity is kind of a long time. The average human has an eighty-plus-year life-span. Some humans have been known to live a little past one-hundred years. But in the grand scheme of things, this is a pretty short amount of time.

Let's say you know someone who is a horrible person. From their teenage years on, they have been an angry, hateful individual. Then, at the ripe old age of ninety-three, they die (because we all know angry, bitter people live longer). This means this person was a mean and nasty pain in the ass for seventy-some-odd years. How long should they be tortured after they die?

The correct answer is zero. No one deserves to be tortured—not for five minutes, not for fifty years, not one hundred years. No one deserves to be tortured for a thousand years or a million years, and certainly no one deserves to be tortured for all eternity for finite transgressions.

Even in the flawed justice system of the United States, convicted felons are allowed the opportunity to receive parole or reprieve from their sentences. The extremely flawed American justice system acknowledges that people can change. Their sentences can be reduced if the offended have shown they have reformed from their offending ways or have demonstrated good behavior while incarcerated.

Sure, there are many different religious believers out there who try to make up the rules of hell in order to make it a more palatable concept. The general rule is that unless you are saved here on Earth, you are doomed for all eternity. Basically, the rule is "Once damned, always damned." God's divine justice is much less nuanced than the obviously imperfect justice system of the United States.

There are only one-way tickets to hell, and apparently there are highways that go there too. Souls go in, but they don't go out.

If you put this in the context of time, you can easily see the problem. Again, in most cases, we live fewer than one hundred years, and yet, if we do not swear allegiance to God or swear allegiance to the wrong God on insufficient evidence, we will allegedly be tortured for more than a trillion years, all with no hope of reprieve or parole.

This is obviously unfair and immoral, and that is why we are seeing many Christians today trying to distance themselves from the concept of hell in some way or another. Many Christians have tried to tell me that hell isn't eternal torture after all, that hell is a good thing.

Yeah, God takes everyone who loves him to paradise in heaven, and everyone else can just opt out. Hell is really just opting out of Paradise City. But then there is the fine print. God is love, so without God, there can be no love. So by opting out of heaven, you are opting out of love, and your existence will be filled with the Dementor's Kiss from the Harry Potter series. Because, hey, if that is your choice, who is God to stand in the way of your desire to opt out of love and live an eternity of hopeless despair? It isn't like he is some all-powerful deity who created the rules and the power to change them at his whim or anything, right?

The thing is that, according to Christianity, there are truly only two choices. If you reject Christianity, or even if you reject the "True" Christianity, you are "choosing" to be tortured for all eternity without any chance for parole. Christians can call that torture an "opt out," a rejection of God's love, or whatever gentle euphemism they like, but it all amounts to the same horrific punishment for not believing ridiculous claims on insufficient evidence.

Of course, there is that other "choice," in which you choose to believe the ridiculous claim of the one "True" Christianity on insufficient evidence. Then you get rewarded for all eternity. You get to walk up that lovely staircase to heaven and frolic with the angels and judge contests to see how many of them can dance on the head of a pin. Heaven is loads of fun . . . or is it?

Well, Muslim heaven isn't much fun. They get seventy-two virgins. But since eternity is, as discussed earlier, an extremely long time, that is about one virgin every few trillion years or so. That's even less sex than many Islamic fundamentalists get on Earth—although it is probably more sex than Christians get in heaven. Still, it isn't exactly what they expected. And what those homophobic Islamists don't realize is that those virgins might actually be dudes.

But heaven is no picnic for Christians either. When you think about it, who really does want to live forever? Sure, life is too short and it can move pretty fast, but if you had all the time in the world, or in this case, more than all the time in the world, what would you do?

First, we have to take all the sins off the table because there is no sinning in heaven. So scratch out sex, eating, drinking, gambling, killing zombies, science, and watching *Game of Thrones*. Anything worth doing is forbidden in heaven.

Then we have all the other things we could do in heaven. How quickly will that get boring? After a while, Justin Bieber is going to get very annoying—and by a while, I mean ten seconds.

Seriously, though, there is a lot of time to fill in eternity. You take out all the fun stuff and what can you really do? Maybe you can watch your loved ones get tortured in hell. Maybe there is a cable station in heaven called Hell TV where you get to see all the people you loved and cared about who prayed to the wrong deity, or no god at all, get tortured. How fun would that be? Then again, that might be considered wrath.

It seems to me that even heaven is a bit of a hell. In fact, when you think about it, heaven might even be a fate worse than hell. At least in hell you will be with all the cool people like Gandhi, Susan B. Anthony, Albert Einstein, Jimmy Hendrix, George Carlin, Christopher Hitchens, Joan Rivers, and Bruce Lee.

4. You Just Don't Know

Let's face reality here for a moment. There is no valid evidence for any deities. If there was valid and compelling evidence, then we would all be on the same page. There wouldn't be a million sects of each religion, and there wouldn't be a million different religions. There would be one sect of one religion, and God would make his presence known to us in a way that was so obvious and unambiguous that it couldn't be disputed. We would be able to see him, hear him, smell him, touch him, and so on. There would be no atheists because God would present to each of us the precise evidence we would need to be convinced that he was real. After all, he's God, and he could do that kind of thing.

No, that doesn't affect our alleged "free will." I know that Kim Jong-Un exists, but you don't see me worshiping him. Just because we would know that God exists doesn't necessarily mean that we would choose to follow him, obey him, and/or worship him.

I am often told that God is all-powerful and that should be reason enough to worship him. I disagree. For starters, there is no evidence that this all-powerful deity even exists. A threat that Voldemort will curse me if I don't worship him won't compel me to worship him because I don't believe Voldemort actually exists. Second, even if God or Voldemort were proven to exist (or at least there was some compelling evidence for their existence), I still wouldn't worship them, and I hope you wouldn't either.

When believers say this type of thing, it tells me more about the believer's lack of moral fortitude than it does their faith-based convictions. My point is that I don't worship based on how powerful a being or meta-being is alleged to be.

I remember mentioning this to a fundamentalist Christian friend of mine in college, and she completely missed my point. Paula argued that in the end, I don't really have a choice to worship her God at all. She quoted a Bible verse at me: "For it is written, As I live, saith the Lord, every knee shall bow to me, and every tongue shall confess to God" (Romans 14:11).

More threats from a deity that I still don't even believe exists. And this is where Pascal makes his infamous and ridiculous wager. First a Christian will assert that we can't really know whether God exists or not. So isn't it better to believe in the biblical God than not believe? After all, if Christians are correct and you do believe, then you would go to heaven and avoid hell. On the other hand, why take the chance that there isn't a God and risk not only being barred from entrance to heaven but also getting a one-way ticket to hell to be tortured for all eternity with no chance for parole or reprieve?

Because, at the end of the day, religious believers with all their faith-based certainty are quick to become momentary agnostics if they think it will win them a convert. Still, truth be told, they are right about one thing: there is no actual physical evidence either way.

There could be some deity out there who doesn't really interact with the world and as such cannot be detectable with any human-designed equipment or with any human-designed tests. Such a deity, however, would most assuredly not be the deity described in the Bible. That god allegedly interacts with the world all the time and has even taken the liberty of designing a test that could prove or disprove his own existence. But I'll get to that later.

Even without a physical test, I think I have shown through logical argument with the previous essay that God does not exist. But for the sake of illogical argument, let us pretend together that logical arguments aren't enough to disprove God. Like I said before, there is no physical evidence one way or the other. At the end of the day, we don't know with absolute certainty that a god of some sort doesn't exist somewhere in some form.

Of course I also can't rule out the possibility that Darth Vader didn't really exist a long time ago in a galaxy far, far away. I would need a time machine and a starship that could make the Kessel Run much faster than twelve parsecs. Wait a minute, that's not even a unit of velocity!

My point is that Darth Vader might exist. Or more accurately, he might have existed. We can't be certain that he didn't. Still, for all practical reasons, no one would have a problem declaring that Darth Vader is a fictional character. No one claims to be agnostic about the existence of Darth Vader. Could you imagine if they did? Everyone would laugh at them. The same is true of God. I might not know with absolute certainty that God doesn't exist, but for all practical purposes, the probability that a god does exist is extremely low to the point where I feel reasonably certain and pretty darn comfortable saying that God is a fictional character created and revised over time by ancient people to answer questions they could not answer themselves.

In strictly definitional terms, it makes sense to admit that we are all in fact agnostics in that we lack knowledge of the existence of any deities. But from strictly definitional terms, believers and unbelievers both must also admit that we lack knowledge about the existence of Darth Vader or Voldemort. Yet interestingly enough, no one talks about their uncertainty or lack of knowledge concerning these two figures. And for the record, Darth Vader finds your lack of faith in him disturbing.

No, when we talk about our knowledge about various things in everyday life, we talk about our practical knowledge, and it is assumed that we are speaking about reasonable certainty rather than absolute certainty. At the end of the day, we don't know about anything with absolute certainty. For all we know, we could just be some computer simulation playing on an alien iPad. We just don't know.

But . . . there is always a but. We can know with some degree of high probability that the God character in the Bible is completely fictional. Unlike Darth Vader, God doesn't live far, far, away. God is supposed to be right here, right now. God is supposed to be able to do amazing things, like suspend the laws of nature. And according to the Bible and most religious believers, God answers prayers. These are all things we can test and have in fact tested.

Scientists have tested the effectiveness of prayer many times over the years. In most cases, those who have been prayed for have at best slightly better recovery rates. In most cases, the recovery rates for those prayed for and those not prayed for have been statistically the same. And in one study, those prayed for actually did slightly worse than those not prayed for. Still, no study has shown that prayers changed recovery rates significantly.

We would expect that if God exists and if prayers to him actually worked, then (1) those who prayed to the correct deity regularly wouldn't even have health problems in the first place and (2) prayers to the correct deity would significantly increase a believer's recovery rate. I mean, we'd expect nearly 100 percent of those prayed for would recover instantly.

But we don't see that. What we see is that prayers don't work. It doesn't matter which god you pray to, or how many people pray to that god, or what the intentions are of the people praying. The recovery rate is about the same as it is for atheists and those not prayed over. Still, we can't say with certainty that God doesn't exist.

On the other hand, author Marshall Brain makes a great point in his book *How "God" Works: A Logical Inquiry on Faith*. In the book, Brain calls attention to the biblical passage in 1 Kings 18.

In this passage, the prophet Elijah is skeptical about the god Ba'al. He demands a test. Elijah asks the 450 prophets of Ba'al to bring forth two bulls. They are to cut the bulls up and put them on two separate woodpiles. But instead of lighting the woodpiles to cook the bulls, they are each to pray to their deity to light their respective woodpile.

Elijah even mocks the followers of Ba'al as they pray to their deity of choice with no results. Of course, after a fashion, Elijah decides that it is time for him to pray to his God, the God of the Bible. In the story, God lights Elijah's fire and thus proves his existence. Elijah then slaughters the followers of Ba'al mercilessly for worshipping a false god. But that is beside the point.

The point is that in the Bible, Elijah created a test to prove that God is real. If Elijah can test God, why can't you or I test God? Let's ask God to do something impossible. On the next sunny day when there are no clouds in the sky and the meteorologists aren't expecting any chance of thunderstorms, ask God to light your barbeque grill for you so that you can cook your hot dogs and hamburgers. Don't even equip the grill with a propane tank or charcoal. Just pray and let God do his thing. While you're doing that, I'll pray to the god of science and hook up that full propane tank.

Still, even if nothing happens and God doesn't light your fire, that doesn't prove anything. Maybe God hates you. Maybe he just doesn't like hot dogs and hamburgers. Maybe he has become a vegetarian. Maybe you didn't pray correctly or in the right direction or he doesn't like to be tested by you. It might not be in his divine plan to cook your dinner, or maybe he just works in mysterious ways. Again, at the end of the day, we can't really know if God exists or not with absolute certainty.

But that's alright. As a science-minded humanist, I am OK with not knowing everything. As an atheist, I don't need to know with absolute certainty that God doesn't exist. I just need to lack the belief that he does exist. And it is easy to lack belief in something when there is no valid evidence supporting the existence of that thing. Not only is there no valid evidence supporting the existence of a god, but there is evidence that at least makes one think that God doesn't exist, such as the ineffectiveness of prayer, the randomness of wealth and disease, and the fact that God failed to light your fire. He failed the barbeque test.

All that being the case, I feel pretty darn comfortable with my lack of belief, and yet I still remain open to the possibility that I don't know everything and that I could be wrong. I guess, if you wanted to get technical about it, you could label me as an agnostic atheist, but for all practical reasons, I'm reasonably certain that God does not exist.

The thing is that I am willing to admit that I don't know with certainty. How many religious believers are willing to make that admission sincerely?

5. The Bible Is Ridiculous

Have you read the Bible? I mean *really* read it and not just flip around to the pages that your religious leader told you to or watched some miniseries on television telling you their version of the stories. I don't know why, but those shows always leave out the best parts. Where are the zombies? When Jesus was crucified on the cross, the Bible says that there were earthquakes and zombies: "Jesus, when he had cried again with a loud voice, yielded up the ghost. And, behold, the veil of the temple was rent in twain from the top to the bottom; and the earth did quake, and the rocks rent; And the graves were opened; and many bodies of the saints which slept arose, And came out of the graves after his resurrection, and went into the holy city, and appeared unto many" (Matthew 27:50–53). What television producer in their right mind would leave out the most interesting part of that story?

The thing is that the Bible is filled with this kind of stuff, like when God sent two bears to maul forty-two children for calling a guy "bald." Don't take my word for it; be skeptical. It's right there in 2 Kings 2:23–24: "And he went up from thence unto Bethel: and as he was going up by the way, there came forth little children out of the city, and mocked him, and said unto him, Go up, thou bald head; go up, thou bald head. And he turned back, and looked on them, and cursed them in the name of the LORD. And there came forth two she bears out of the wood, and tare forty and two children of them."

Unfortunately, aside from the surprisingly large number of hilariously ridiculous stories like these, the Bible is pretty boring. And that is probably why so few religious believers have ever actually read it. The sheer number of things like dull, contradictory lists of genealogies and conflicting accounts of the same events is sure to put the most hard-core insomniac to sleep.

Let me just say this: There is a reason the Bible is the most recommended book by atheists. That reason is that it is boredom peppered with absurdity.

As the old saying goes, the devil really is in the details. Take a good look at some of your favorite Bible stories next time you are sitting in church or synagogue bored to tears. The book is right there. And you can read it to show just how much of a devout believer you are. I bet you'll be surprised by what it actually says.

But it's not just the details, like God needing to create a woman from a man's rib while able to create the entire universe out of nothing. No, the preposterousness is also in the stories themselves—at least that's the case with Christianity. Perhaps nowhere is this clearer than in the need for Christ in the first place.

Here we have a story where God has to fix his mistake through a super-elaborate scheme involving impregnating a married virgin, waiting thirty-three years, allowing his son / himself to be murdered, and then waiting three more days before resurrecting himself bodily to heaven, witnessed by no one but his friends and one skeptic who didn't seem all that skeptical to me given the situation.

Plus, when you think about it, no one—not even his fan club—actually "saw" Jesus bodily rise from the dead. They just assumed that he did because they couldn't find his body. I don't know about you, but that probably wouldn't have been my first assumption. Besides, everyone knows what they say about "assuming" stuff, right?

To put it in perspective, if magician David Blaine came back from the dead on live television, we would all applaud, but I doubt anyone would think it was anything other than a really good trick. For the record, there were no televisions back then, and Jesus didn't even resurrect himself bodily in front of a live audience; he allegedly did it behind a rock in a sealed cave. To make the situation even more questionable, the Gospels give very different accounts of who was actually there . . . and by "there," I mean there after it had already allegedly happened.

Getting back to my point, it seems kind of silly to me that God would have to allow his son / himself to die at all. What is he, a vampire or something—in need of blood? How else do you explain the blood fascination?

It's morbid and super-creepy. God will forgive you for any crime you ever commit, but he needs the blood of an innocent lamb to make it right. Come to think about it, lamb's blood is kind of weak sauce—even if the lamb was innocent. So let's step it up a bit and go with God's own divine blood. But since deities don't bleed, best make myself a human being first, then I can bleed myself silly for your sins.

On what planet does a story like that make any kind of sense? Oh, right, this one apparently.

CONCLUSION

I've lost track of the number of times I have been reunited with a religious believer whom I once long ago had religious discussions with either online or in person and they came back to me and casually mentioned that they no longer believe in God. Oh, it usually wasn't something I said that suddenly deconverted them—at least not directly—but my contribution was certainly one scenic stop on their road to superstitious abandonment. In many cases, it may even have been their first stop.

In college, this was so common that one Fundamentalist Christian friend jokingly called me a "soul murderer." She didn't mean that literally, of course, since she believed souls were immortal and cannot die, let alone be murdered. But her point was that due to me, someone whose soul had been saved would now have their soul doomed for all eternity to be tortured in agonizing pain in hell.

Religious believers don't just hear a rebuttal of their favorite arguments or have the "Truth" of their holy and inerrant Bible shown to be in error and then suddenly lose their lifelong faith. That's not how believers become atheists. Many religious believers usually have had some semblance of religious education, whether formally or informally, and then have had society reinforce their religious beliefs. There is an indoctrination process that often starts before they can even walk or talk. Even if someone grows up in an atheist household with atheist parents, there is still societal indoctrination. In America today, there are more churches in a town than there are drug stores, banks, or any other single type of business. Oh yes, churches are businesses—and very profitable ones at that. Plus, they don't even have to pay taxes. But I digress. My point is that religion is all around us and is a constant presence in our culture. Breaking away from that is not easy.

Religious conversions are quick. Someone has had this exposure to religion in the background of their lives even if they grew up with atheist parents. However, most Americans have grown up with a casual reverence for religion and maybe some mild religious lip service—that is, if they did not grow up in a full-blown religious household where the indoctrination was completely overt. Whatever their situation, they have already been primed. Then some kind of emotional experience happens . . . something that elicits a feeling of helplessness, fear, or grief and maybe, on rare occasions, joy. This might even get them thinking about death or mistakes they have made in life. While this person is in this vulnerable state, someone comes over and tells them about this new drug called Jesus and— boom—instant religious conversion.

But atheism isn't like that. Atheism is a thoughtful journey. It takes a lot of time and critical thinking before a religious believer can overcome all the societal indoctrination. It takes even longer for that person to not just accept the fact that they no longer believe but vocalize it to others. We live in a judgmental world, and few are more judgmental than those who quote Bible verses about not being judgmental.

Recently converted "Born Again" religious believers are quick to talk about their newfound faith, but recently minted atheists often keep their lack of faith quiet out of fear of losing friends and/or family.

I hope this book will help start that long journey for some religious believers and give atheists some new material to share with religious believers in their lives. I hope that a religious believer will read this book, toss it aside, and say, "That was a stupid argument, and the cases this Staks guy made for atheism were just silly." Then that religious believer will go and tell all his or her friends about that stupid atheist book *Disproving God*.

The religious believer will then continue with his or her life, going to church or Bible study or whatever, and then suddenly think . . . *Wait a minute, that thing in the Bible doesn't make sense. I must have interpreted it incorrectly. And wait, did my pastor say that? The Bible says this. Let me look that up. Let me look this up. Let me Google this and check out a library book on that. Let me argue with an atheist about this and talk to my religious leader about that.*

OK, I want the religious believer to say to him- or herself, *maybe I got it wrong. Maybe I should be interpreting the Bible this way instead of that way.* Then I'm hoping that the believer will realize that for all these reinterpretations of verses and passages, the whole thing is just fiction. That maybe, just maybe, God doesn't exist and that ancient people who still thought the world was flat made up stories to help them make sense of things. Then maybe I'll get an e-mail or social media message saying, "Hi, a few years ago, I read your book *Disproving God* when I was a Christian, and I was thinking about it the other day and thought I would let you know that I'm an atheist now and that this book was one of the stops on my journey."

****

Thanks for reading this short book. I truly hope you enjoyed it or will at least think deeply about it. It would really mean a lot to me personally if you could take a moment to leave a review at your favorite retailer and/or send me a personal note with your thoughts and comments. I love talking to both atheists and believers about the values we hold deeply, even if they are diametrically opposed.

Thanks again!

—Staks

ABOUT THE AUTHOR

Staks Rosch is an atheist activist, writer, blogger, and former talk radio host. He is the former head of the Philadelphia Coalition of Reason (PhillyCoR) and has served on the board of the Freethought Society of Greater Philadelphia.

As creator and host of the Dangerous Talk Radio Show, Staks discussed atheism, politics, and social issues. The show later transitioned to the Freethought Radio Podcast Network alongside The Infidel Guy and The Rational Response Squad.

As a writer, Staks was the National Atheism Examiner on Examiner.com, served as a *Huffington Post* contributor, and worked as a freelance writer for *Publishers Weekly*'s Religion section. He continues to blog on the SkepticInk Network (SIN).

Feel free to follow him on Twitter @ DangerousTalk and "Like" the DangerousTalk Facebook group. Let's continue the journey together.

Printed in Great Britain
by Amazon

61532395R00037